FRED THE FARTING GINGERBREAD MAN

Written and Illustrated by Drew Dally

Copyright 2022 Drew Dally Publishers.
ISBN: 978-1-959581-03-1

All Rights Reserved. No part of this book may be reproduced in any form without permission in writing from the publisher.
All inquires about this book can be sent to the author at
drewdallybooks@gmail.com

In a cottage far away lived an old woman and man.
They had no children, but the old woman had a plan.
With an apron and baker's hat too, she baked gingerbread and no longer felt blue.

With gumdrop buttons and icing all **around**,
Fred was the sweetest in **town**.
He baked in the oven all the way **through**,
and when done, he shouted, **"Peekaboo!"**

The old lady gasped in **fright**.
He was bright and small in **height**.
Fred ran in a flickity **flash**
and hoped he wouldn't **crash!**

He stuck out his tongue and sang with his lungs, "I am faster; my farts are a blaster!"
He squeezed and out came a flippity-farty flarrrrrp! He shot like a rocket, and the couple couldn't stop it. "Come back!" they shouted, but Fred pouted, "Never!"

In the grassy fields was a kooky-crazy cow.
He wanted to eat Fred too, so Fred had to leave now!
He hid behind a cheesy-bees tree,
but the cow could still see
Moooo!

The cow opened its mouth, and Fred passed **gas**: blrrrrappp!
The smell was so bad, the cow's face turned **green!**
The biggest flubble-bubble it had ever **seen!**

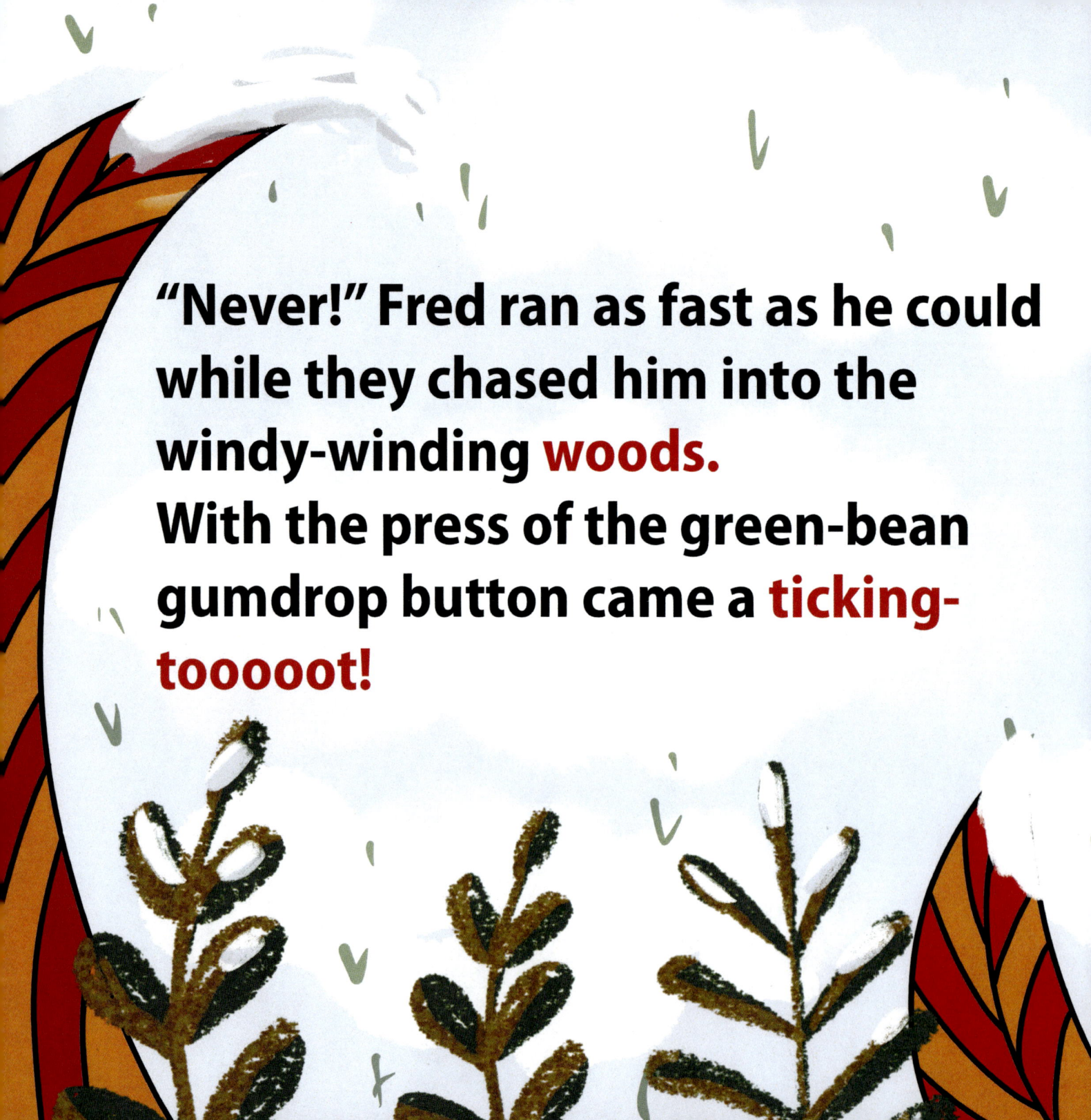

"Never!" Fred ran as fast as he could while they chased him into the windy-winding woods.
With the press of the green-bean gumdrop button came a ticking-tooooot!

A cloud of smoke poofed out of his **butt** and was not **cute!**
It was so loud and **big,**
it woke up the wiggly-giggly **pig!**

"Oink, oink, let me eat you!" the pig said.
"Shoo-shoo!" It would not budge. What else could he do?

Fred pressed the blue gumdrop button,
and out came a pooooot!
The stinky, dinky gas sounded like a flute!
The flarpy-fart flew him from the couple,
the cow, the horse, and now the pig,
but then he flew toward a chicken in a wig!

They still wanted to eat him, so he pressed the yellow gumdrop button and flew on a **whim.**

Brrrrrap! Frrrrap! Blrrrrap! The flarpy-farts flung him like a **slingshot.**
He was so fast and couldn't **stop!**
Pfffffft, poooosh! Soaring through the sky, the gas bubble was right behind. The stench was so foul, it made everyone **sick!**
Fred looked back. "That did the **trick!**"

He flew to a friendly, furry fox. "Hi, can you help me escape?"
"Sure, I'll put on my cape!" The fox flew, and there was nothing they could do.
"You can see up high on my head!" the fox suggested.
Fred hopped onto the fox's head for a view but had no clue.

Chimp-chomp! The fox ate Fred with a crack! Crunchy and sweet, what a delicious snack!

Even though Fred's farts were smelly, that didn't stop the fox. He liked the smell of the eggs and stinky, smelly socks!

THE END

Made in the USA
Middletown, DE
05 December 2022